KU-539-952

Museums and Historic Houses

Midlanders are fortunate in having a wide variety of museums and historic houses liberally spread throughout their region. As schools and colleges increasingly involve the student in learning about his environment, so the museums and historic houses can prove increasingly helpful.

Making full use of an exciting selection of forty photographs and line drawings, the authors provide a gazetteer of more than one hundred and twenty Midland museums and historic houses.

The Midlands is not solely a factory and foundry complex with its roots entrenched in the industrial revolution. It has a history developed from Prehistoric and Roman times. The museum collections reveal evidence of life from those periods and can, by displaying current plans of city development, give a glimpse of the Midlands of the future.

The authors show how the museums gather their materials, mount their displays and provide a genuine service for schools, colleges and the Midlander making an intelligent use of his leisure time.

For all who have an interest in the Midlands this book is a valuable source of reference.

"THIS ANIMAL WAS CALLED THE TRICERATOPS PRORSUS."
"NOT TO ITS FACE, I PRESUME."

WAYLAND REGIONAL STUDIES

THE MIDLANDS

Museums and Historic Houses

Michael and Anna Meredith

WAYLAND PUBLISHERS LONDON

More Midland Books

13737

DY

SL
069.09424
MER

[914.240485]

700185

069
9424

SBN 85340 320 1
Copyright © 1973 by Wayland (Publishers) Ltd
101 Grays Inn Road London WC1
Printed by Garden City Press Ltd Letchworth Herts

Contents

List of Illustrations

Museums

Museums vary in size, shape and content. Some of them were set up to house collections of paintings, sculpture and other works of art and are known as art galleries. Other museums concentrate on interests such as natural history, archaeology, local history or science and industry. Sometimes art gallery and museum are combined under the same roof.

Some old houses have been preserved more or less as they were when people lived in them. They include great houses generally known as "stately homes," and smaller dwellings which are preserved for their architectural interest or for their connection with famous people.

Another type of museum concentrates on transport and veteran cars, trams, or trains are displayed – sometimes under cover and sometimes in the open air. And old buildings are often collected together on the same site to form museums of architecture.

In addition, certain firms have built up their own museums to show the history of their development and products.

Many museums and historic houses belong to local authorities, although a number are also run by private individuals and other miscellaneous bodies. The National Trust, for example, plays a very important part in preserving historic buildings, and it has opened over two hundred of them to the public. The Government also looks after many buildings, ancient sites and museums. This is the work of the Department of the Environment. There are also a number of services museums, which are usually run by army regiments.

Right This eighteenth century squire's marriage coach, known as the Beaumanor Coach, can be seen as Leicester Museum.
Below Sheffield's last tram takes visitors to the Tramway Museum at Crich for a ride.

WOLVERHAMPTON TEACHERS
COLLEGE LIBRARY

Museums of the past

Before the eighteenth century most collections in Europe were private. Often their owners collected rarities for social prestige, or because they believed ancient objects had magic powers. For example, Egyptian mummies were a very popular item. They were said to "restore wasted limbs, cure consumption, ulcers and all manner of other bodily complaints."

During the seventeenth and eighteenth centuries, however, private collectors such as Ferrante Imperato of Naples and Sir Hans Sloane began to emphasize the pursuit of knowledge. Objects were catalogued systematically, and information and ideas were exchanged with other scholars. Often these collections had a very wide scope. In 1733, Sir Hans Sloane's collection of nearly seventy thousand items consisted of books, cameos, seals, coins and medals. But there was no attempt to display exhibits to make them look attractive or easier to understand.

After the death of Sir Hans Sloane, his collections were opened to the public in the New British Museum in 1759. However, things were still far from perfect. The intending visitor had to apply for a ticket two weeks in advance so that his credentials could be vetted. Children under ten were not admitted. Rapid tours of the museum were organized, but there were very few labels and the guides frequently had no time to answer the visitors' questions.

Museums, therefore, were still cabinets of curiosities, and few people tried to gain admission to the British Museum. They much preferred the displays of strange and rare items in London coffee-houses, or the exhibitions like Mr. Bullock's Egyptian Hall. Here, in 1822, vast numbers came to view a mermaid which was nothing but the head and shoulders of a monkey sewn on to the tail of a large fish! In time, more and more museums and art galleries

RITRATTO DEL MVSEO DI FERRANTE IMPERATO

Above The crowded interior of Ferrante Imperato's private museum. There is no attempt at an orderly display and visiting scholars focus their attention on single specimens that are of interest to them.

were founded. The National Portrait Gallery, for example, was opened in 1896, and in the provinces the municipal galleries of Birmingham, Liverpool and Manchester became important before 1900. They were open daily, even on Sundays, so that working people could easily visit them. Admission fees were low or non-existent.

Behind the scenes

The head of a museum is usually called the director or curator. Those directly under him are in charge of different sections of the museum, and are generally known as keepers. The keepers are responsible for purchasing and cataloguing new material. They carry out research and look after the objects in their care. They also arrange displays and exhibitions. In larger museums they are helped by assistant keepers and they often take charge of smaller branch museums. At Birmingham Museum, for example, the Keeper of Archaeology looks after the archaeology collections in the main museum together with an eighteenth century water mill, a half-timbered house and the site of a medieval manor.

Today, museum displays are arranged to look attractive and to help the viewer learn more about the world around him. Bright colours, modern materials and exciting layouts are used. Designers are sometimes engaged, either on the permanent staff or part time, to help the keepers arrange gallery interiors, displays and exhibition lay-outs. They also design museum booklets and posters.

Various technical staff play an important part in running museums. They may be qualified taxidermists, who stuff dead animals for exhibition. Or they could be employed to mount or frame prints and pictures. Other staff are in charge of cleaning and repairing ancient embroideries and costumes.

Much of the work of running a museum isn't at all glamorous. Bills have to be paid, the exhibits have to be insured, salaries and wages have to be calculated. In some museums the director will see to this with help from clerical and typing staff but, in larger ones, an administrative officer will supervise.

Again, in larger museums, education officers may be employed to help young people, school parties, teachers and the general public.

The material displayed in the showcases only forms a small part of the museum's collections. The rest of the objects, known as reserve collections, are kept in store until the time when they are to be put on display again or are needed for research. Usually museums try to change their displays as often as is practical, so that the public can see different selections of objects.

Below A conservation technician at Birmingham Museum builds up a medieval pot. The work of the technical staff is behind the scenes, but it is very important.

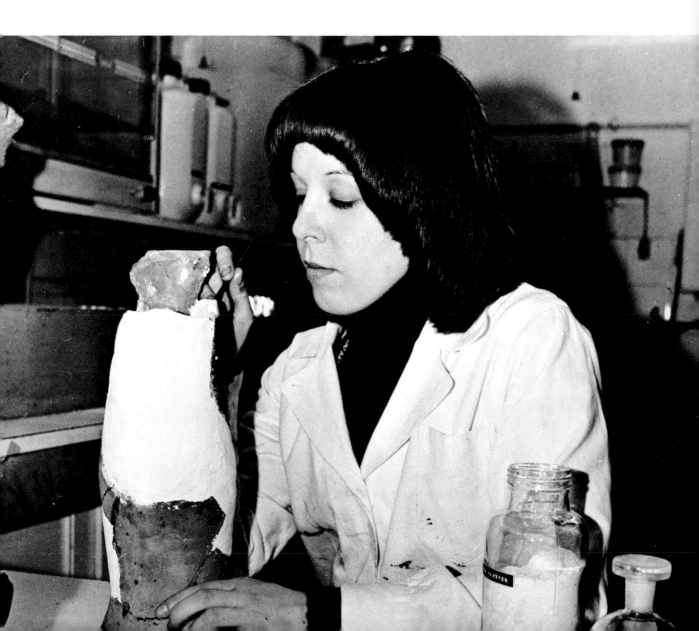

Right A member of the Birmingham Museum staff records birdsong at the Earlswood Nature Trail. Recordings are often used to make make natural history displays more realistic.

Exhibits

How does the museum obtain its exhibits? Some of them are bought, but most museums have surprisingly small purchase funds. Many are given by members of the public or bequeathed in wills. Often material is loaned, sometimes permanently.

Nobody goes out any more to shoot birds and animals for natural history displays. Frequently the public bring in victims of road accidents or pesticides and, if they are not already too decayed, they are stored in the museum's deep freeze until the taxidermist has time to deal with them. If they have been stored in suitable conditions, old specimens, even those dating back to Victorian times, can be given a new lease of life by a skilled taxidermist and then incorporated in new displays. Fish, snakes, reptiles and amphibians are often

14

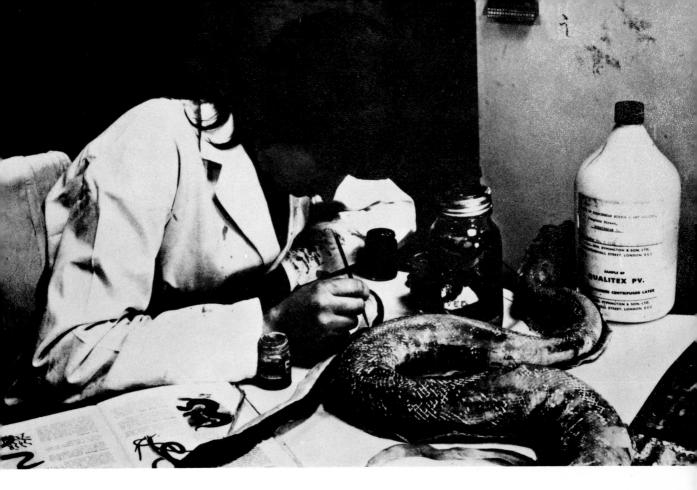

skilfully moulded from the real thing using liquid *latex*.

Much of the archaeological material will come from digs in the immediate local area. Items from abroad are bought, or obtained by subscribing to exploration societies.

Most museums run by local authorities are paid for out of the rates, the national ones are paid for by the government and some are run by trusts. Many stately homes are run for profit by their owners, who rely on the proceeds of admission fees to maintain their estates. The National Trust is a charity and relies on donations, subscriptions and admission fees.

Above A technician carefully paints the cast of a snake in the laboratory of Birmingham Museum and Art Gallery.

Clubs and societies

Often museums hold temporary exhibitions to supplement their permanent displays. Sometimes these are organized by the museum concerned, or they may be arranged by other bodies or museums. The Victoria and Albert Museum, for example, has a policy of arranging numerous travelling exhibitions from its reserve collections.

Clubs and societies for all ages are often run by museum staff. "Friends of the Museum" societies usually combine fund raising with social functions based on the museum or art gallery. Sometimes, in the case of open-air museums, there is a chance to give practical help in restoring buildings and machinery. Often there are natural history and archaeological societies, which have junior sections or provide family membership.

Some museums, especially those with education officers, run young people's clubs. These provide a chance to learn more about the collections and to carry out creative work in the museum itself. Recently a museum invited children between eight and fifteen to study cave paintings and prehistoric implements. They then did their own cave paintings on high, corrugated cardboard "cave" walls. The resulting "caves" were displayed in the public galleries.

Lectures about the collections and allied topics are provided for both adults and children. Some larger museums hold them at regular intervals, perhaps once a week, during the lunch hour. Serious students are allowed to study the reserve collections if they write and ask in advance.

Most museums have an "opinions service." The staff try to identify objects brought in by the public, although they are not allowed to estimate their value in money. Occasionally old oil paintings do turn out to be old masters!

Publications produced by museums range from detailed catalogues of the collections to attractive illustrated booklets and postcards. Quiz booklets, badges and historic costume dressing dolls are produced for young people.

Not all the museum's activities take place indoors. Field excursions for those interested in geology and archaeology are arranged and some museums even run their own nature trails.

Below Holiday activities at Birmingham Museum. After studying cave paintings and prehistoric implements, the children concentrate on decorating their own cave walls.

School Museums

Egyptian Burial Customs

The Egyptians thought that when they died they would go to a world like this one and that their body would still be needed, so they carefully preserved it by drying and bandaging. It was put into a brightly painted coffin which had a lid with a human face painted on it (a). Internal parts like the stomach and lungs were removed and put in special containers called Canopic Jars (b).

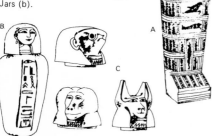

These are made of stone and come in sets of four, each with a different lid (c). One shows an ape called Hapi, one is a man called Imsety. The dog is called Duamutef and the hawk is Qebeh-sen-uef. The Egyptians thought that they might have to work in the Afterworld and so they provided model servants who would do the work for them. They carry tools and a basket and often have the man's name written on them in hieroglyphs. They are called by their Egyptian name, Ushabtis (d).

While they were bandaging the body the Egyptians put in a number of small charms or amulets, to protect it. A special scarab (e) was placed near the heart and a pendant (f) on the chest.

Some schools have built their own museum collections. One Midland school studied metalwork in local museums. Their own museum grew remarkably quickly. Items ranged from seventeen flat irons and charcoal irons to a miner's lamp and a pair of glass working tongs. Everyone who brought an object completed a card for the card index. Information included a description, details of the donor, the place and date of finding, and material extracted from books and local sources. The cards were filed in a catalogue and a label was made for the museum display. Then older people in the area were asked about their memories of life in the past. As a result old photographs, and information about local history and folklore, were discovered.

Schools undertaking projects like this can be given considerable help from museum staff, especially in identifying their finds. At the same time some of their discoveries may eventually form a welcome addition to the museum's collections.

Left Museums produce a wide range of publications for children and many special exhibitions are arranged *(right)*. This "Please Touch" exhibition provides the opportunity to take a closer look at the specimens.

Gazetteer of Museums and Historic Houses

Both the historic houses and the museums are listed under counties. Addresses and telephone numbers (where possible) are given. In brackets are the names of the organizations, or individuals, who own and run the properties. All museums closely grouped are branch museums of the first entry in the group. Before arranging a visit it is advisable to write or telephone to check on opening times and admission charges. For information about the National Trust properties, telephone 01-930 0211.

Below Kenilworth Castle in the sixteenth century.

Above A modern exhibition on health education is clearly and neatly displayed at Birmingham Museum. At the end of the nineteenth century, in contrast, the displays were usually very crowded *(right)*.

Derbyshire

DERBY MUSEUM AND ART GALLERY, Strand, Tel. 31111, (Derby Corporation). The museum contains antiquities, *bygones*, coins, medals, zoology, *geology*, transport and local exhibits. There is a Bonnie Prince Charlie room which is associated with the 1745 Rebellion.

The art gallery contains costume, Derby porcelain and paintings. There is an education department which arranges holiday activities for young people.

DERBYSHIRE COUNTY MUSEUM, Sudbury Hall, Sudbury, near Derby, DE6 5HT, Tel. 028-378 305, (Derbyshire County Council). This museum concentrates mainly on exhibits of interest to young people —such as toys, games and costume.

KEDLESTON HALL, Derby, Tel. Derby 840386, (Viscount Scarsdale). The present house, though originally Stuart, was re-designed during the mid-eighteenth century for Nathaniel Curzon, 1st Lord Scarsdale. To achieve a better visual effect, the old village which stood in front of the house was removed.

James Paine, one of the foremost architects of the period, was at first employed to re-style the house. By 1761, he had constructed the north front with its six *Corinthian* columns rising above a double staircase. In 1760 the famous architect and designer, Robert Adam, was commissioned to work with Paine. The house is now one of the finest examples of Adam's work in England. His love of *classical* design is evident in the south front which was inspired by the Arch of Constantine in Rome, in the hall with its twenty Corinthian columns of green-veined Derbyshire *alabaster*, and in the circular saloon which recalls the Pantheon in Rome.

Within the house are displayed silver-ivories,

weapons, and other treasures collected by the Marquess when he was Viceroy of India, from 1898 to 1905. Notable amongst the eighteenth century furnishings are two pieces by Adam's cabinet maker, John Linnell – a mirror with its carved and gilded frame of palm tree motifs breaking the glass into several sizes, and a sofa also of carved gilded wood with an exotic design of a triton, or river god, supporting the head-rest. Included in the collection of paintings is Rembrandt's *Daniel interpreting Nebuchadnezzar's Dream.*

Below A passenger train passes the engine shed and coaling plant in the Midland Railway model at Derby Museum and Art Gallery.

Derbyshire

MELBOURNE HALL, Melbourne, Tel. Melbourne 2502, (The Marquess of Lothian). The original sixteenth century hall was developed by Sir John Coke (1563–1644), often referred to as "the last Elizabethan." It was enlarged and considerably altered in the eighteenth century.

Besides housing an important collection of pictures, furniture and *objets d'art*, the house is famous for its formal gardens by William Wise, the royal gardener to William III, Anne and George I. The gardens, with their avenues, fountains and statues, are in the French style of André le Nôtre who designed the gardens at the Palace of Versailles. In contrast is the wrought-iron bird cage "pergola," designed and constructed by a local blacksmith, Robert Bakewell of Derby. His work may also be seen in All Saints Cathedral, Derby, and the Radcliffe Camera, Oxford.

Many famous people are associated with the house. It was the home of the nineteenth century Prime Minister, Lord Melbourne, from whom the Australian city took its name in 1837. Lord Byron's friend, Lady Caroline Lamb, lived there, and Lady Palmerston inherited the estate.

SUDBURY HALL, Sudbury, near Derby, DE6 5HT, Tel. 028-378 305, (National Trust). The hall, formerly belonging to the Lords Vernon, is a seventeenth century red brick house. It was begun in 1613 by Mary Vernon and completed by her son, George (1670–1695). The exterior is notable for its "grand front" by Sir William Wilson, the central doorway of which displays *Baroque* influence. The rooms are furnished in the style of Charles II's reign and contain work by three of the outstanding craftsmen of their period–murals by Louis Laguerre, a carved staircase by Edward Pierce, and an overmantel by Grinling Gibbons. There are also some fine plasterwork ceilings.

TRAMWAY MUSEUM, Crich, near Matlock, Tel. Ambergate 2565, (The Tramway Museum Society). The open air museum contains a unique collection of horse, steam and electric tramcars and associated equipment. Trams can be seen in operation. The tramway was built by volunteer members of the Tramway Museum Society.

Below The long gallery at Sudbury Hall. Notice the elaborate plasterwork ceiling.

Leicestershire

BELVOIR CASTLE, near Grantham, Tel. Knipton 262, (Duke of Rutland). The house is situated between Grantham and Melton Mowbray, overlooking the Vale of Belvoir. It has been the home of the Dukes of Rutland since the time of Henry VIII. The former fortress was rebuilt during the seventeenth century but, circa 1800, James Wyatt was commissioned to reconstruct the house as a castle. Wyatt rebuilt the south-east wing, raised the height of the Stanton tower, added a new range of buildings, and constructed a further round tower. After a fire in 1816 the north side was rebuilt by James's sons, Benjamin and Matthew Wyatt.

The interior includes the long Regent's gallery in the south-west wing, which contains a series of busts by Joseph Nollekens. The rebuilt east tower was designed by Sir John Thoroton, a relative of the family, and contains the Elizabeth saloon with its life-size statue of the 5th Duchess and painted ceilings, both by Matthew Wyatt. Other rooms were designed by Benjamin Wyatt in French *Rococo* style, which was soon popular everywhere. Besides pictures by Holbein, Reynolds, Gainsborough, and other notable artists, there are two of particular local interest—the portraits of the 4th Duke and Duchess by the rector of nearby Knipton, the Rev. William Peters (1742–1818).

LEICESTER MUSEUM AND ART GALLERY, New Walk, LE1 6TD, Tel. 26832-3-4, (Leicester Corporation). There are paintings and ceramics together with biological and geological exhibits. The museum holds archives including borough and archdeaconry records.

BELGRAVE HALL, Thurcaston Road, Tel. 61610. This furnished Queen Anne house (1709–13), and gardens, has stables with coaches and agricultural collections.

Above A portrait of Mary Isabella, Duchess of Rutland by the Reverend William Peters.

GUILDHALL, Guildhall Lane, Tel. 21523. This was a medieval Guildhall and later Town Hall of Leicester. There is a hall, mayor's parlour, library and cells.

JEWRY WALL MUSEUM, St. Nicholas Street, Tel. 22392. The exhibits include the Roman Jewry Wall and baths, and a mosaic pavement.

MUSEUM OF TECHNOLOGY, Abbey Pumping Station, Corporation Road, Tel. 61330. The road transport gallery contains horse-drawn vehicles, cycles, motor cycles and motor cars.

NEWARKE HOUSES MUSEUM, The Newarke, Tel. 50988-9. The museum illustrates the social history of the city and county from 1500 to the present day. There is a period street scene, costume, local clocks, and exhibits relating to the hosiery industry.

RAILWAY MUSEUM, London Road, Stoneygate. There are items relating to local railway history including four locomotives.

Above A life-size painting of Charles, fourth Duke of Rutland by the Reverend William Peters.

Leicestershire

MARKET HARBOROUGH ARCHAEOLO-GICAL AND HISTORICAL SOCIETY MUSEUM, The County Library, Tel. 2649. This contains the collections of the Market Harborough Archaeological and Historical Society.

STANFORD HALL, near Rugby, Tel. Swinford 250, (Lord and Lady Braye). The site has belonged to the Cave family, the ancestors of Lord Braye, since 1430. The present house was begun by William Smith the Elder (1697–1700) and was finished between 1730 and 1745. Many Stuart pictures and relics are displayed, besides antique furniture, old kitchen utensils, and family costumes dating back to the reign of Elizabeth I.

In the stables (built in 1737) is a collection of vintage motor cycles and motor cars. There is a full size replica of the 1898 Flying Machine of Percy Pilcher, a pioneer aviator killed at Stanford during trials in 1899.

STAPLEFORD PARK, near Melton Mowbray (Lord Gretton). The house displays a mixture of architectural styles. The oldest part dates from circa 1500, and was built by Thomas Sherard. Its decoration depicts scenes from history, legend and the scriptures. A 1633 "restoration" saw the addition of Flemish gables, and further alterations were made both in 1670 and during the Victorian period.

The interior contains rooms attributed to John Webb and an interesting collection of paintings, tapestries and furniture. In the grounds stands the eighteenth century parish church, with a fifteenth century brass and two marble tombs. One is from circa 1732, and is the work of the famous sculptor, Rysbrack. Of particular interest is the Thomas Balston Collection of nineteenth century Staffordshire portrait figures. Many of these were sold at fairgrounds. The collection specializes in famous people–Victoria and her family, Victoria with

Above Percy Pilcher was the first man to fly in England. His experimental work was carried out at Stanford and a replica of his flying machine can be seen at Stanford Hall.

her Crimean War allies, incidents from campaigns, celebrated generals, statesmen, preachers and theatrical personalities. These were the popular heroes and themes of the Victorian era.

Northamptonshire

ALTHORP, near Northampton, Tel. East Haddon 209, (Earl Spencer). The Spencers have lived here since 1508. The original house was altered in 1573, again in 1666, and lastly in 1790. Here Anne, wife of James VI of Scotland, stayed on her journey to London to hear her husband proclaimed James I of England in 1603.

The house contains pictures from many European Schools, a large collection of European and Oriental porcelain, and eighteenth century English and French furniture. Many of the pictures by Italian and Dutch masters were collected by Robert Spencer, 2nd Earl of Sunderland, who died in 1702. He also panelled the

The romantic setting of Rockingham Castle inspired Charles Dickens *(left)* to use it as a model for Chesney Wold in *Bleak House*.

Picture Gallery which displays portraits by Van Dyck, Lely, Kneller and other artists. In the Marlborough room is the personal collection of Sarah, 1st Duchess of Marlborough. Her daughter married into the Spencer family, and her descendants succeeded to the Marlborough title. They often retained the name Spencer, as in Winston Spencer Churchill.

NORTHAMPTON CENTRAL MUSEUM AND ART GALLERY, Guildhall Road, Tel. 34881, (Northampton Corporation). The museum houses collections of footwear through the ages and a cobbler's shop. The archaeological material is local and there is a collection of English *ceramics*. Oil and water-colour paintings are on show.

ABINGTON MUSEUM, Abington Park, Tel. 31454. This is a fifteenth century manor house, partly rebuilt in 1745. There are period rooms, including a small replica of a Victorian street scene. Displays include *ethnographical*, natural history and folk material.

ROCKINGHAM CASTLE, near Corby, (Commander L. M. M. Sanders Watson). The original royal fortress and hunting base was begun in Rockingham Forest by William I. The *Norman* gateway and keep, some twelfth century outer walls, and the banqueting hall from the reign of Edward I can still be seen. In 1554, the castle was granted by Henry VIII to Edward Watson, ancestor of the present owner. Within the older remains stands a house, mainly Tudor and Elizabethan, although other additions have been made from time to time. The romantic setting of the ruins inspired Charles Dickens to use it as a model for Chesney Wold in *Bleak House*. There is a good collection of eighteenth, nineteenth and twentieth century English paintings.

Right The inauguration of George Washington as first President of the United States. The design of the Stars and Stripes flag is believed to be taken from the Washington family coat-of-arms, which can be seen at Sulgrave Manor.

Northamptonshire

SULGRAVE MANOR, near Banbury, Tel. Sulgrave 205, (The Sulgrave Manor Board). Sulgrave is a small Elizabethan manor house, completed circa 1560 by Lawrence Washington, an ancestor of George Washington, first President of the United States. It was Colonel John Washington, George's great-grandfather, who left England during the Civil War to settle in Virginia in 1656. The design of the Stars and Stripes flag is believed to have been taken from the Washington family coat-of-arms, which may be seen carved on the stone porch above the main doorway. It consists of three horizontal stars above two horizontal bars or stripes. The house itself, partly rebuilt between 1920 and 1930, is basically Elizabethan with some Queen Anne additions. On display are a number of portraits and possessions of George Washington. The great kitchen is remarkable for its collection of antique equipment.

THE WATERWAYS MUSEUM, Stoke Bruerne, near Towcester, Tel. Northampton 862229, (British Waterways Board). The museum contains canal boat relics, photographs, maps, documents, and traditional boat-folk possessions. These include their nineteenth century costume, and a large collection of decorative crochet and lace-work from boat cabins.

Right This old photograph of boatmen can be seen at the Waterways Museum. Like most men who worked on the canals, these two are wearing corduroy trousers, brass buttoned waistcoats with velvet collars and braided braces.

Nottinghamshire

MANSFIELD MUSEUM AND ART GALLERY,
Leeming Street, Tel. 22561 Ext. 64, (Mansfield Town Council). The museum houses zoological specimens, pottery and local water-colours.

NEWARK CASTLE (Newark Corporation). This former stronghold on the main route to the North, where King John died in 1216, was dismantled in 1646 when the Royalist cause was lost. The impressive ruins comprise the north and west walls of the castle, still relatively intact, with the three corner towers and a fourth tower in the middle of the west wall. In the latter, arches and windows of Norman, *Gothic* and Tudor styles can be seen.

NEWARK MUSEUM AND ART GALLERY,
Appleton Gate, Tel. 2358, (Newark Corporation). The museum contains local archaeology and history, with some natural history and art. Especially interesting are two seventeenth century coin hoards and some Anglo-Saxon cremation urns.

Nottinghamshire

NEWSTEAD ABBEY, Linby, Tel. Blidworth 2822, (Nottingham Corporation). A priory was founded on this site, circa 1170, by Henry II as an act of penance for the murder of Thomas Beckett, Archbishop of Canterbury. Some traces of this building may still be seen. Following the Dissolution of the Monasteries the abbey was bought by Sir John Byron, in 1540, and converted into a house. It remained the family seat until 1818 when Lord Byron, the poet, sold it to pay his debts. During the nineteenth century the house was reconstructed in Gothic style, following designs by John Shaw.

The house displays Byron relics, including some rare editions of his poems. There are also paintings, some Tudor and Stuart furniture, and a collection of English armour. Among the portraits is the famous painting of Byron by Thomas Phillips. Byron's bedroom, next to a supposedly haunted room, displays a large four-poster bed, though it is questionable whether the poet slept in it very much as he spent little time at Newstead. He merely wrote tersely of the house that it "spoke more of the baron than the monk." He did, however, intend to be buried here and share the tomb of his favourite dog, Boatswain. This is to be seen in the terraced gardens, occupying exactly the site of the high altar of the former priory church. A further interesting monument is housed in the crypt dedicated to "Little Sir John Byron (died 1604) with the great beard." The explorer David Livingstone wrote his book *The Zambesi and its Tributaries* while staying at Newstead in 1864–65.

NOTTINGHAM ART GALLERY AND MUSEUM, The Castle, Tel. 43615, (Nottingham Corporation).

Left This portrait of Lord Byron, by Thomas Phillips, hangs in the Byron dining room at Newstead Abbey.

The museum specializes in ceramics (especially medieval earthenware and Nottingham stoneware). There are also local antiquities, notably medieval alabaster carvings which were made around Nottingham. There are collections of textiles, embroideries, paintings and drawings.

NATURAL HISTORY MUSEUM, Wollaton Hall, Nottingham, Tel. 281333. This Elizabethan mansion houses the Corporation of Nottingham's natural history collections. There are zoological, botanical and geological sections.

INDUSTRIAL MUSEUM. This is a new museum in the stables of Wollaton Hall. It features Nottingham industry, with special reference to lace-making.

Above This beehive honeypot, by the great silversmith Paul Storr (1771–1844), can be seen at Nottingham City Museum.

Nottinghamshire

NOTTINGHAM CASTLE (The Duke of Newcastle, leased to Nottingham Corporation). The original castle was a wooden fortress, built during the reign of William I. It was rebuilt in stone at the beginning of the twelfth century, but soon after was burned down. The building was reconstructed by Henry II, who bequeathed it to King John. During this period it was the centre of the bitter feuds which are immortalized in the legends of Robin Hood. In 1212, for example, King John, furious at the news of a further Welsh rebellion, hanged at Nottingham twenty-eight youths who were being held as hostages for the good conduct of their fathers.

A century later Edward III's mother, Queen Isabella, lived in Nottingham Castle with her favourite, Roger Mortimer. But, in 1330, they were arrested by the young King and his soldiers, who secretly entered the castle by a passage still known as "Mortimer's Hole." The castle has many other famous connections. Owen Glendower was imprisoned there, Edward IV proclaimed himself King and denounced Warwick "the Kingmaker" at Nottingham, and Richard III occupied the castle before the Battle of Bosworth. The fortifications were finally dismantled by Cromwell's troops during the Civil War.

In the late eighteenth century, a new building was constructed in *Italianate* style by the Duke of Newcastle. However, in 1831, it was burned by Luddite rioters because the Duke persistently blocked the proposed political reforms. It was then restored, and is now leased to Nottingham Corporation to house the City Museum and Art Gallery.

THORESBY HALL, Ollerton, (The Countess Manvers). The house, set in a splendid park, was built by Anthony Salvin in Neo-Tudor style between 1864 and 1875. The main features include a three-storied

Right The great hall at Thoresby Hall. Notice the structure of the hammerbeam roof and the fine mantelpiece.

great hall with *hammerbeam roof*, and an entrance tower modelled on Burghley House in Northamptonshire. The principal rooms have decorated ceilings and floors and wall panelling of oak, walnut or maple. There are some fine carved mantelpieces in white marble. The Library chimney-piece, for example, depicts a scene in Sherwood Forest. The hall also houses the Frank Bradley Exhibition of Toy and Model Theatres.

Nottinghamshire

THRUMPTON HALL, Nottingham, Tel. Gotham
333, (George Fitzroy Seymour). The property was
owned for six hundred years by the Powdrill family, but
they were dispossessed after the Gunpowder Plot of
1605. One of the conspirators, Father Garnett, was
concealed in a priest hole which was built into the
chimney breast at the foot of a staircase. In 1607 the
Pigots took possession, and the original house was
almost totally rebuilt as a Jacobean manor house. It was

further enlarged between 1660 and 1669, and again between 1827 and 1835–this time in Gothic style. There is a fine example of a *Jacobean* carved staircase, and some notable pictures and furniture. During the nineteenth century a niece of the owner married a descendant of the poet Byron, and the house displays some Byron relics.

WOLLATON HALL, Nottingham, Tel. 281333, (Nottingham Corporation). This is a fine example of late Elizabethan *Renaissance* architecture. It was built between 1580 and 1588 by the architect Robert Smythson, for Sir Francis Willughby. Smythson had assisted in the rebuilding of Longleat in Wiltshire, and he attempted a similar style, but with further elaboration, at Wollaton. From the centre of the house rises a great hall, which has projecting turrets at the four corners. The *façade* and sides of the house have *Ionic* pillars, rich mouldings, and large windows—one for every day of the year, according to tradition.

The interior of the great hall displays good examples of a carved stone screen and a hammerbeam roof. For many years the paintings of the north staircase and the ceiling of the south staircase were attributed to Antonio Verrio (1639–1707), but research has now established them as the work of Louis Laguerre (1663–1721) and Sir James Thornhill (1676–1734).

WORKSHOP MUSEUM, Memorial Avenue, Tel. 2408, (Worksop Corporation). There are displays illustrating local history, archaeology and natural history.

Left The east front of Wollaton Hall.
The house was built for Sir Francis
Willughby at the end of the
sixteenth century.

Rutland

LIDDINGTON BEDE HOUSE, Liddington, Tel. Oakham 822438, (Department of the Environment). The house is an interesting example of a medieval Bishop's palace which has been converted into a seventeenth century almshouse. The building was erected by Bishop Russell of Lincoln (1480–96) and Bishop Smith (1496–1514). In 1602 the palace was slightly adapted when Thomas Cecil, the son of Lord Burghley, Queen Elizabeth's Treasurer, converted it to an almshouse "for twelve men and two women!" Persons receiving such charity were obliged to pray for their benefactors. This is the origin of the name Bede House. It comes from the old English word "biddan," which means to pray.

On the upper floor, the former banqueting hall of the palace has a fine ceiling with carved *cornice*, wooden panelling and original windows. Many parts of the building have been restored.

RUTLAND COUNTY MUSEUM, Catmose Street, Oakham, Tel. 3654 (Rutland County Council). The museum contains archaeological objects, local history material, craft tools and agricultural implements.

Shropshire

ATTINGHAM HALL, Atcham, near Shrewsbury, Tel. Upton Magna 202, (National Trust). The Hall, in classical style, was built in 1784 from designs by George Steuart. Its slender columns and long colonnades are typical of the elegance of the late eighteenth century.

In 1807, John Nash was commissioned to build a picture gallery. He constructed it in materials which were not commonly used at this time—iron and glass. The internal decoration is in the style of Wyatt. Much of the furniture and pictures, such as the Louis XVI and Empire furnishings of the drawing room, were collected by the third Lord Berwick when he was Minister at Naples. There are paintings by Caravaggio, Salvator Rosa and representatives of the Venetian, Veronese and Spanish Schools.

Left The Georgian interior of Attingham Hall, with its slender columns, is typical of the elegance of the late eighteenth century.

Shropshire

BENTHALL HALL, Much Wenlock, Tel. Telford 882659, (National Trust). The house is built in stone, with brick chimneys and mullion windows, and dates from the late sixteenth century. On the façade are four discs which were arranged, so tradition maintains, to represent the stigmata (Christ's wounds on the cross) by the Catholic owners – the Benthall family. During the seventeenth century there were alterations to the interior, but a richly carved oak staircase (circa 1610) survived. It has *baluster*-shaped *newel posts* and bold *finials*. In the parlour beyond the staircase there is some original plaster panelling, plastered beams and a finely decorated *frieze* of animals in *roundels*.

BOSCOBEL HOUSE, Shifnal, Tel. Brewood 850244, (Department of the Environment). Boscobel House was built early in the seventeenth century for John Giffard, who planned to use it as a place of hiding for persecuted Catholic priests. There have been extensive alterations over the centuries, although there is some early seventeenth century panelling and a little plasterwork. One of the hiding places, in the chimney stack in the main chamber upstairs, is now thought to be an earth closet. The other priest hole is situated below a trap door at the head of the attic stairs.

Boscobel's most famous association, however, is with Charles II. Here, after the Battle of Worcester in 1651, Charles spent a day hidden in an oak tree. The King and Major William Careless remained aloft while the servants of the house, five brothers named Penderel, kept watch. This account of Charles's escape from the Parliamentary troops was first published in 1660, in Thomas Blount's *Boscobel*. But, unfortunately, as soon as the fame of the Royal Oak spread souvenir hunters went to work. By 1706, according to John Evelyn, the tree had been killed by people hacking at the bark. A tree sown from an acorn of the original now stands

His face you see. Now briefly hear the rest;
How well he served his Prince in flight distressed.
Twas he whose little household did combine
In pious care to save : the Royal Line.
An oak was thought most safe; for what could prove
More lucky than the sacred tree to love.
See where the hen-roost ladder stands; by that
The mighty monarch climbed the boughs of state,
Where noble Carlos lent his manlike knee,
The last support of fainting majesty.
And nature's tapestry was the only shroud
To shelter the great prince with rage pursued.
The nut-hook reaching up its homely fare
Supplied the want of waiters standing bare;
While busy wife and children gather wood
To dress the sheep prepared for better food.
Thus many oaks defend the British main
But one preserved the British sovereign.
Pendrill thy name will shine in history
Brighter than theirs, whose hospitality
Disguised deities hath entertained,
For thine was real to other poets fained.

Left The Royal Oak of Boscobel House. This was the tree in which Charles II hid from Cromwell's troops, as the poem *(far left)* tells.

in its place. The memory of the escape is perpetuated by Oak Apple Day on May 29th (King Charles's birthday), and by the countless inn signs bearing the picture of the Royal Oak, often with Charles or his crown in the branches.

Shropshire

IRONBRIDGE GORGE MUSEUM, Church Hill, Ironbridge, Telford, Shropshire, TF8 7RE, Tel. Ironbridge 3522, (Ironbridge Gorge Museum Trust). The Ironbridge Gorge Museum is a new open air museum, which is being created around a unique collection of monuments of the Industrial Revolution. At the Coalbrookdale Museum, and Darby furnace site, are the remains of the seventeenth century blast furnace where Abraham Darby first smelted iron with coke. There are also exhibits, such as street furniture and locomotives, which illustrate the history of iron smelting and casting. Near the museum stands the oldest iron bridge in the world. It was built from iron

Left The oldest iron bridge in the world was built from iron smelted at the Coalbrookdale factory, in 1779.

44

smelted at the Coalbrookdale foundry, in 1779. The Blists Hill Open Air Museum on the Coalport road has a display of steam engines, blast furnaces, and pithead gear. There is also an historic stretch of canal and the remains of a tile works.

LUDLOW CASTLE, Ludlow, (Earl of Powis). The castle dates from the eleventh century, when work was begun by Roger de Lacy, but building continued into the sixteenth century. Today the twelfth century circular chapel, the tower, and the great hall stand out from among the ruins.

The castle was fortified for Matilda during the Civil War which shook England between 1135 and 1154. In 1138 Stephen besieged Ludlow but the castle's defender, Gervase Paganel, held off his attacks. Edward IV lodged his two sons here—Edward and Richard, better known as the "Princes in the Tower." The elder, Edward, was actually proclaimed King at Ludlow on his father's death, but the two brothers were soon removed to the "safety" of the Tower. Henry VII's eldest son, Arthur, brought Katherine of Aragon to Ludlow Castle for the first few months of their marriage. Within a year Arthur had died, and Katherine was betrothed to his brother, the future Henry VIII. There are many other royal connections. For example, Mary I lived here for a few years before she was Queen. This was one of the few happy times in her life. The castle also has its literary connections. John Milton's play, *Comus*, was first performed here in 1634.

During the Civil War Ludlow was garrisoned by Royalists, and the castle only submitted after all the other strongholds in the country had fallen. Its fortifications were then dismantled.

WOLVERHAMPTON TEACHERS
COLLEGE LIBRARY

Shropshire

LUDLOW MUSEUM, Butter Cross, Tel. 2619, (Shropshire County Council). The museum possesses a fine collection of fossils. There is also local material dating from prehistoric, Roman and medieval times, including arms and armour.

PLAISH HALL, Church Stretton, (Messrs. Tristam Gilbert and C. A. du Guay). Plaish Hall, built in the reign of Henry VIII, is the earliest recorded brick building in Shropshire. The greater part was built by Sir William Leighton, Chief Justice of North Wales. The most remarkable feature of the building is the collection of early Tudor brick chimneys. The story is told of how Justice Leighton passed sentence of death on a master builder, and then discovered that the man was a renowned craftsman in brickwork. The sentence was consequently suspended, on the understanding that the craftsman would construct a set of chimneys for the Justice's house which no other builder could imitate. The builder, hoping to obtain a pardon, surpassed himself in the execution of this task. Nevertheless, he was duly hanged on the completion of the work.

There is an interesting ceiling in the house, which is divided into panels by thin ribs and decorated with emblems of "H.R." (Henricus Rex) and early Renaissance scrolls. The walls have Elizabethan panelling. An effigy of Justice Leighton lies in nearby Cardington Church.

SHREWSBURY ART GALLERY, Castle Gates, Tel. 52255, (Shrewsbury Corporation). The art collections are limited to those of local (Shropshire) interest.
CLIVE HOUSE, College Hill, Tel. 54811. This is a fine Georgian house containing a collection of Shropshire ceramics. Art, furniture and geological specimens are also on display. The Regimental Museum of The First the Queen's Dragoon Guards is housed here.

COLEHAM PUMPING STATION, Old Coleham, Tel. 52255. This contains two compound rotative beam engines, built by Renshaw of Stoke-on-Trent and installed in 1900.

ROWLEY'S HOUSE MUSEUM, Barker Street, Tel. 52255. There is a fine collection of Roman material from Viroconium (Wroxeter), together with medieval and prehistoric remains.

Below The drawing room ceiling at Plaish Hall is divided into panels and decorated with emblems of H.R. The Hall was built during the reign of Henry VIII *(left)* and the letters H.R. stand for Henricus Rex.

Shropshire

STOKESAY CASTLE, Craven Arms, (Lady Magnus Allcroft). In the twelfth century the site of the house was owned by the de Saye family. The name was later Anglicized to Stokesay. Parts of the building, which is a fortified manor house, date from the thirteenth century. These include the north tower, which is surmounted by later timber work, the great hall and the *solar*. The south tower, sixty-six feet high and nearly forty feet across, was added in 1291 when a licence permitting further fortification was granted to the owner, Lawrence of Ludlow. His descendants lived in Stokesay until 1497. A half-timbered gatehouse was added circa 1570. In 1645 the Royalist owner of the

house, Lord Craven, was besieged, and compelled to surrender. The curtain walls were removed, but otherwise the house was left intact. It did, however, fall into decay during the first half of the nineteenth century. It was acquired by the Allcroft family in 1869.

VIROCONIUM MUSEUM, Wroxeter, (Department of the Environment). Objects found during the excavation of this Roman city are on display. These include an important Roman inscription from the forum, pottery, coins and other small objects. Viroconium was originally a legionary fortress but it became the major town, Viroconium Cornoviorum, of the Cornovii tribe.

Left A drawing of Stokesay Castle by Edward Blore (1787–1879).

Shropshire

WENLOCK PRIORY, Much Wenlock, Tel. 466, (Department of the Environment). A Saxon nunnery, founded about 680 by St. Milburga, a Mercian princess, originally stood on this site. In 896, it was sacked by the Danes. Later, Lady Godiva founded a college for priests here, but this was demolished during the Norman Conquest. The ruins which can be seen today are those of the twelfth century foundation of Roger de Montgomery, Earl of Shropshire. As a Cluniac priory it was under the jurisdiction of the French foundation of La Charité-sur-Loire. After the French Wars of the thirteenth century it was penalized for these ties, which were finally broken in 1395. The destruction of the priory was the work of Henry VIII's soldiers during the Dissolution of the Monasteries.

The remains, mainly Early English in style, are considerable. The surviving south transept, for example, still rises to a height of seventy feet. There are some fine examples of Norman carving, both on the interlaced arches of the chapter house and on a panel of the cloister *lavatorium*, which depicts Christ asleep in the boat on the lake.

A miraculous story of the Norman foundation is told by the twelfth century chronicler, William of Malmesbury. During the construction, the body and tomb of St. Milburga were discovered and a scent of balsam spread through the church. Soon, so many miracles were performed that the crowds of pilgrims could scarcely be contained. But, by the seventeenth century, Thomas Fuller, the antiquarian and chaplain to Charles II, was more sceptical. "In the reign of William I," he wrote, "her body was taken up sound and uncorrupted to the admiration of the beholders. This I am sure of, that as good a saint, Lazarus by name, by the confession of his own sister, did stink when but four days buried."

Some fine examples of Norman carving are to be found at Wenlock Priory. *Below* Two of the apostles.

50

WESTON PARK, near Shifnal, Tel. Weston-under-Lizard 207, (The Earl of Bradford). The house was built by Lady Wilbraham in 1671, and is a good example of the *Restoration period*. The pictures include works by Holbein, Van Dyck, Reynolds and Gainsborough, and there are French tapestries from the Gobelin and Aubusson factories. There is some seventeenth century silver and many letters written by the Victorian Prime Minister, Benjamin Disraeli, who was a frequent visitor. The gardens and park, designed by Capability Brown, include a temple of Diana by James Paine.

Below A detail from the cloister lavatorium at Wenlock Priory, showing Christ asleep on the waters.

Shropshire

THE WHITE HOUSE COUNTRY LIFE MUSEUM, Aston Munslow. This fourteenth century, *cruck*-built, manor house exhibits dairying and domestic utensils. Agricultural tools and horse-drawn implements can also be seen in their functional setting.

WILDERHOPE MANOR, Wenlock Edge, (National Trust). The manor, built of limestone, was begun in 1586 and has remained unaltered except for the addition of some plaster ceilings in the seventeenth century. The house was originally owned by the Small-wood family, one of whom gave his name to the nearby "Major's Leap" on Wenlock Edge. During the Civil War, Major Thomas Smallwood, hotly pursued by Roundheads, turned his horse over the Edge and was saved by grasping a tree protruding from the side. The horse plunged to its death, but the Major escaped and delivered his message.

The most elaborate of the seventeenth century plaster ceilings is to be seen in the parlour. This has ribs which form star patterns. There is also a motto in plasterwork which is in keeping with the Royalist associations of the family—*Droit Dev est Mal Mev*, or "Due Right is Ill Disturbed."

Staffordshire

BLITHFIELD HALL, near Rugeley, Tel. Dapple-heath 249, (Lady Bagot). Blithfield has been the home of the Bagot family since 1086. The present grey stone hall is basically Elizabethan. It was built by Richard Bagot, enlarged in the eighteenth century, and Gothicized about 1820. There is a seventeenth century carved oak staircase, many family portraits, and some Stuart relics which include an embroidered satin cap worn by Charles I.

Family coaches are displayed in the stables and the gardens include an eighteenth century orangery. Visitors may also see the famous herd of goats descended from those given to Sir John Bagot by Richard II. Here, each year, on a Monday early in September, the Abbots Bromley Horn Dancers perform the famous dance which is said to commemorate the hunting rights once enjoyed in the adjacent Needwood Forest.

Visitors to Blithfield Hall today can see the famous herd of goats descended from those given to Sir John Bagot by Richard II *(right)*. Richard became King in 1377 and was forced to abdicate by his cousin, Henry Bolingbroke, in 1399.

Staffordshire

BLITHFIELD HALL MUSEUM OF CHILDHOOD AND COSTUME, Blithfield Hall, near Rugeley, Tel. Dapple Heath 249, (Lady Bagot). There are exhibitions of children's books, toys, furniture, miniature theatres, Georgian costumes and uniforms.

BURTON-UPON-TRENT MUSEUM AND ART GALLERY, Tel. 3042, (Burton-upon-Trent Corporation). This contains local history material and travelling art exhibitions.

CENTRAL ART GALLERY, WOLVERHAMP-TON, Lichfield Street, Tel. 24549, (Wolverhampton Corporation). Eighteenth and nineteenth century English water-colours and oil paintings, including works by Gainsborough and Fuseli, are on display in this gallery. There are also modern prints, paintings and drawings, and an Oriental collection.
BANTOCK HOUSE, Bantock Park, Tel. 24548. The house contains a fine collection of English painted *enamels* and *Japanned* ware. There are also collections of dolls, Royal Worcester porcelain, Wedgwood and Staffordshire pottery.
BILSTON MUSEUM AND ART GALLERY, Mount Pleasant, Tel. 42097. This museum has some fine examples of English painted enamels and Staffordshire pottery.

CHEDDLETON FLINT MILL, near Leek, (Cheddleton Flint Mill Industrial Heritage Trust). Twin water wheels on the River Churnet operate flint grinding pans. There is a collection of machinery used in pottery milling.

E. M. FLINT ART GALLERY, Lichfield Street, Walsall, (Walsall Corporation). The gallery houses a number of paintings and a collection associated with

Jerome K. Jerome (1859–1927), humorist and author.

A lock collection is on show in neighbouring Willenhall, the home of the lock and key industry since Elizabeth I's reign.

GLADSTONE POTTERY MUSEUM, Uttoxeter Road, Longton, Stoke-on-Trent, Tel. 39232, (Staffordshire Pottery Industry Preservation Trust). This museum is housed in some old "bottle-oven" kilns, and aims to show the history of the pottery industry. It will be opening to the public in the late spring of 1974.

LEEK ART GALLERY, Nicholson Institute, Tel. 2615. (Leek Corporation) There are small permanent art collections here, which are supplemented by travelling exhibitions.

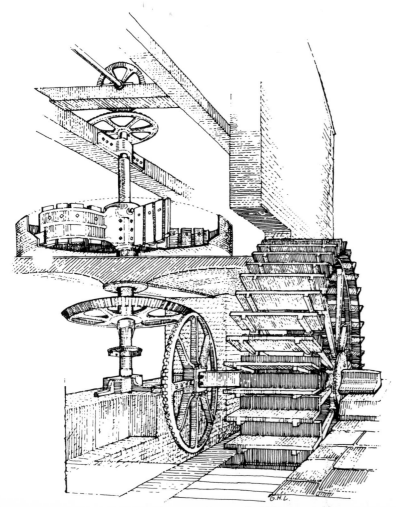

Left The North Mill at Cheddleton, near Leek. The mill was built some time before 1783, and the waterwheel is 22 feet in diameter and 5 feet $9\frac{1}{2}$ inches wide.

Staffordshire

LETOCETUM MUSEUM, Wall, Tel. Shenstone 480768, (Department of the Environment). Finds from the excavated Romano-British settlement of Letocetum, and from nearby Shenstone, are on show. The remains of the Wall bath house are more complete than those of any similar bath house found in Britain.

LICHFIELD ART GALLERY AND MUSEUM, Bird Street, Tel. 2177, (Lichfield Corporation). The museum specialises in local history. The art gallery shows both loaned and local exhibitions.

DR. JOHNSON'S BIRTHPLACE, 7 Bread Market Street. Dr. Samuel Johnson (1709–84) was famous for the dictionary which he wrote in 1755, and for his work as an author and critic. The house contains relics and pictures of Johnson and his contemporaries.

MOSELEY OLD HALL, Wolverhampton, Tel. Wolverhampton 782808, (National Trust). This was originally a half-timbered Elizabethan house belonging to the Whitgreave family, but it was refaced in brick during the nineteenth century. Here, after nightfall on Sunday 7th September, 1651, Charles II entered the house unannounced after his flight from Worcester. At first the Squire, Thomas Whitgreave, failed to recognize the King, for his hair was cut short and his face was stained with walnut juice. The bed in which Charles slept can still be seen, and so can his secret hiding place. Also displayed are furniture, documents, portraits and other relics of the family.

NEWCASTLE-UNDER-LYME BOROUGH MUSEUM AND ART GALLERY, Brampton Park, Tel. 619705, (Newcastle-under-Lyme Corporation). There are local history collections, which include royal charters, textiles, geology, and eighteenth and nineteenth century water-colours.

THE OAK HOUSE MUSEUM, Oak Road, West Bromwich, Tel. 021-553 0759, (West Bromwich Corporation). This is a sixteenth century, half-timbered house furnished in period style.

SHUGBOROUGH HALL, Great Haywood, Tel. Little Haywood 388, (National Trust and Staffordshire County Council). The eighteenth century hall, the home of the Anson family, now houses the Staffordshire County Museum. The main block was built early in the eighteenth century for William Anson, the father of Admiral Lord Anson. In 1747, the Admiral commissioned the decoration of the "Chinese" room from drawings made in Canton by one of his officers. A Chinese house was also erected in the gardens.

The Admiral's brother, Thomas, employed James "Athenian" Stuart (1713–88), the author of *The Antiquities of Athens*, to add wings to the house and embellish the gardens with ornamental architecture in Greek classical style. Stuart, who was mainly responsible for the revival of the classical style in the eighteenth century, erected four monuments based on his own studies of the antiquities. These were the Triumphal Arch—a tribute to the Admiral—based on Hadrian's Arch at Athens, the Lanthorn of Demosthenes, the Tower of the Winds, and a *Doric* Temple.

In 1803, the architect James Wyatt extended the west front prior to a visit from the Prince Regent. The House is furnished with family possessions, including a fine collection of eighteenth century French furniture and some excellent English examples.

Left Dr. Samuel Johnson, the son of a Lichfield bookseller, was a journalist of considerable talent. He is especially famous for the dictionary which he compiled in 1755.

Staffordshire

SPODE-COPELAND MUSEUM AND ART
GALLERY, Church Street, Stoke-on-Trent, Tel.
48557, (Spode Ltd). The museum has a fine collection
of early Spode blue-printed pottery, bone china, stone
china, and Copeland wares up to the present. Admission
is by appointment only.

STAFFORD MUSEUM AND ART GALLERY,
The Green, Tel. 2151, (Stafford Corporation). Items
illustrating local history, social life, industry and art
are on view. There are loaned art exhibitions.
IZAAK WALTON'S COTTAGE, Shallowford, Tel.
Yarnfield 278. This is the restored cottage of Izaak
Walton, author of the classic *Compleat Angler* (1653).

STAFFORDSHIRE COUNTY MUSEUM, Shugborough, near Stafford, Tel. Little Haywood 388,
(Staffordshire County Council). The museum is in the
former kitchen and stable wing of Shugborough Hall.
There are horse-drawn vehicles, farm equipment,
railway and industrial exhibits, domestic equipment,
pottery, silver and costume. Some geological exhibits
are shown. Occasionally there are craft demonstrations.

Below The Arch of Hadrian was
built in 1770 by Thomas Anson,
as a memorial to his famous brother.

Below A group of tree-fellers from Wheaton Aston, near Stafford, settle down for a meal. This photograph was taken in the summer of 1919 and can be seen in Staffordshire County Museum.

Staffordshire

STOKE-ON-TRENT MUSEUM AND ART GALLERY, Broad Street, Hanley, Tel. 22714–5, (Stoke City Council). This museum contains one of the finest collections of ceramics in the world. It includes English pottery and porcelain, together with Continental, South American, Near Eastern and Oriental pottery. There are also examples of costume, *samplers,* dolls, and Staffordshire archaeological material.

The art gallery contains eighteenth century watercolours and English painting since 1900. Staffordshire birds and animals are displayed in the natural history section.

ARNOLD BENNETT MUSEUM, 205 Waterloo Road, Cobridge, Tel. 25426. This is the early home of Arnold Bennett, the novelist famous for his books about the Potteries. The museum has two rooms of drawings and personal relics.

FORD GREEN HALL, Smallthorne, Tel. 54771. This sixteenth century, timber-framed, manor house exhibits furniture and domestic utensils.

TAMWORTH CASTLE, Tamworth, (Tamworth Corporation). A Saxon fortress built by Ethelfleda, daughter of King Alfred, originally stood on this site. After the Norman Conquest, the land was granted to Robert de Marmion by William I. The keep and massive walls which he had constructed were supplemented with further building by his descendants. The banqueting hall and kitchens date from the reign of Henry VIII. The domestic buildings are mainly Jacobean, and contain some fine examples of woodwork and furniture.

TAMWORTH CASTLE MUSEUM, The Holloway, Tel. 3561, (Tamworth Corporation). The Norman Castle houses a local history museum. Exhibits include the very rare early English coins of the Tamworth mint, armour and weapons.

Above This figure of a mounted soldier was made circa 1745 and can be seen in Stoke-on-Trent Museum.

THE WEDGWOOD MUSEUM, Barlaston, Stoke-on-Trent, Tel. Barlaston 2141, (Josiah Wedgwood and Sons Ltd). The museum has a collection of early Wedgwood pottery. Admission is by appointment only.

WIGHTWICK MANOR, near Tettenhall, Wolverhampton, Tel. Wolverhampton 61025, (National Trust). This half-timbered Victorian house, constructed from designs by Edward Ould between 1887 and 1893, is furnished with original wallpapers and fabrics by William Morris. Also on display are paintings by Rossetti, Millais, Madox Brown and Burne-Jones; water-colours by Ruskin; tiles designed by De Morgan; and some stained glass, by Kempe, which illustrates William Morris's *Earthly Paradise*. The formal terraced gardens were designed by Alfred Parsons, the Victorian painter.

Below These two solid agate ware cats, marbled in white and blue clay, have their ears and eyes picked out in cobalt. They are 4½ inches high and can be seen in Stoke-on-Trent Museum.

Warwickshire

ARBURY HALL, Nuneaton, Tel. Fillongley 40529, (F. H. Fitzroy Newdegate). Arbury Hall, built on the site of an Augustinian priory, has been the home of the Newdegate family since the sixteenth century. The original Elizabethan house was converted into a *castellated* Gothic mansion by Sir Roger Newdegate, between 1784 and 1796. The novelist George Eliot, whose father worked on the estate, conveys an interesting impression of these alterations in her novel *Mr. Gilfil's Love Story*.

Besides period furniture, china, glass, family documents and letters, the house displays some fine plaster ceilings and paintings. Particularly interesting is the portrait of Sir Roger which was painted circa 1762 by Devis. This shows him sitting in the library of Arbury Hall, with the plans for his new house resting on his knee.

The ceilings of the library, drawing room and dining room are outstanding examples of the Gothic style.

The chimney pieces are magnificent. The library chimney piece displays an elaborately pierced *canopy*, with *trefoils*, *pinnacles*, *tracery* and a frieze of grotesque animal heads. The drawing room chimney piece is based on Aymer de Valence's tomb in Westminster Abbey. In the little sitting room is a panel depicting Sir John de Astley's combats with Peter de Masse in about 1438, and Sir Philip Boyle in 1441.

ASSAY OFFICE, Newhall Street, Birmingham, B3 1SB, Tel. 021-236 6951. This houses a collection of old Birmingham and other silver ware, coins, tokens and medals. There is also a collection of the correspondence of Matthew Boulton (1728–1809), the famous Birmingham industrialist and silver manufacturer. Admission is by appointment only.

Right Sir Roger Newdegate sits in the library of Arbury Hall with the plans of his new house resting on his knee.

Warwickshire

ASTON HALL, Aston, Birmingham, B6 6JD, Tel. 021-327 0062, (Birmingham Corporation). As the inscription over the main doorway tells us, this fine Jacobean house was built between 1618 and 1635 by Sir Thomas Holte (1571–1654). He was a man of fiery temper, who is reputed to have split his cook's head from top to chin with a cleaver.

Left Sir Thomas Holte, the builder of Aston Hall.

In 1642, when Charles I was on his way from Shrewsbury to relieve Banbury Castle, Sir Thomas entertained the King at Aston Hall. Later, the house was attacked by a force of one thousand two hundred Parliamentarians. Forty musketeers defended the new hall, but they were forced to surrender. Twelve defenders and sixty Parliamentarians died. The marks of cannon shot are still visible on the walls of the grand staircase, and one of the great carved newel posts was torn away. Two cannon balls used in the conflict can be seen on the first landing. After the capture of the house Sir Thomas was fined and imprisoned.

Members of the Holte family, however, continued to live in Aston Hall until 1818, when it was leased to James Watt, the son of the engineer. It was he who modified the plaster work in the entrance hall. In a letter of 1834 he speaks of repairs and alterations undertaken during his tenancy. His personal device, an elephant, occurs frequently in the decoration.

Since 1864 the hall has been the property of the City of Birmingham, and paintings and furniture in keeping with the period of occupation are now displayed there. There are many eighteenth century embroidered hangings by Mary Holte, and a walnut cabinet which is said to have been presented to Sir Thomas by Charles I. This was given to the City of Birmingham by Mr. Charles Holte-Bracebridge. His family name is used in Washington Irving's novel *Bracebridge Hall*, which was inspired by Aston Hall. The famous football team, Aston Villa, today plays on land which once belonged to the Holte estate.

AVERY HISTORICAL MUSEUM, Soho Foundry, Birmingham, Tel. 021–558 1112, (W. & T. Avery Ltd). The museum displays machines, instruments, records and weights relating to the history of weighing. Admission is by appointment only.

Warwickshire

BARBER INSTITUTE OF FINE ARTS, The University, Birmingham B15 2TS, Tel. 021-472 0962, (Trustees of the Barber Institute). The institute contains a very fine art collection.

BIRMINGHAM MUSEUM AND ART GALLERY, Congreve Street, B3 3DH, Tel. 021-235 2834, (Birmingham Corporation). Birmingham has fine collections of old master paintings and English watercolours. The best known paintings are those by the Pre-Raphaelites, especially *The Blind Girl* by Millais and *The Last of England* by Ford Madox Brown. There are also displays of sculpture, costume, silver and ceramics.

The archaeology department exhibits include material from Ur, Peru, Mexico, Egypt and the Far East. There are prehistoric, Roman and medieval objects. The Pinto Collection of Wooden Bygones is on display.

The extensive natural history collections include animals, birds, minerals and gemstones. The highlights of the geological gallery are the fossil skull of a triceratops dinosaur, and a life size reconstruction of a tyrannosaurus rex.

The museum education department assists teachers and school parties, and runs holiday and leisure activities for young people. The museum also runs a nature trail at Earlswood, just outside the city boundary.
BLAKESLEY HALL, Blakesley Hall Road, Yardley, B25 8RN, Tel. 021-783 2193. This timber-framed house, which dates from the second half of the sixteenth century, contains exhibits dealing with local history.
CANNON HILL MUSEUM, Pershore Road, B5 7RL, Tel. 021-472 0811. The museum exhibits *dioramas*, and illustrates various leisure activities such as bird watching, bee keeping, pets and fishing.

Above This doll, which was made circa 1865, is on display at Birmingham Museum and Art Gallery. The head and arms are made of porcelain and the doll is fourteen inches high.

66

Above Work by Ford Madox Brown (1821–1893).
Below The life-size model of a tyrannosaurus rex at Birmingham Museum.

MUSEUM OF SCIENCE AND INDUSTRY, Newhall Street, B3 1RZ, Tel. 021-236 1022. The museum preserves and exhibits a wide range of objects including steam engines, machine tools, small arms, scientific instruments and veteran cars.

SAREHOLE MILL, Cole Bank Road, Hall Green, B13 0BD, Tel. 021-777 6612. This eighteenth century, water-powered, corn mill is famous for its connection with Matthew Boulton, the Birmingham manufacturer. The mill has been restored and there are exhibits illustrating agricultural pursuits.

WEOLEY CASTLE ARCHAEOLOGICAL SITE, Alwold Road, B29 5RX, Tel. 021-427 4270. The remains of a moated, fortified, dwelling house, constructed between 1100 and 1320, are found on this site. There is a small museum which exhibits the finds.

Warwickshire

CHARLECOTE PARK, Stratford-on-Avon, Tel. Wellesbourne 277, (National Trust). The site has belonged to the Lucy family since 1189. The present house was begun by Sir Thomas Lucy in 1551, and was completed in 1558. Sir Thomas was the landowner before whom Shakespeare was summoned for deer poaching, and whom the playwright later lampooned as Mr. Justice Shallow. The sixteenth century gatehouse, which has remained unaltered, now contains a small museum. The rest of the house was reconstructed during the nineteenth century.

In the great hall are portraits of the Lucy family by such artists as Kneller, Lely and Gainsborough. Over

the chimney piece is a particularly striking picture of Sir Thomas Lucy and his wife taking dessert – Lady Lucy delicately selects a cherry while a nurse holds up the baby. On the chimney piece in the drawing room is a picture of Charlecote dated 1696. This is how Shakespeare would have seen it.

The coach house contains a collection of early carriages, including a travelling coach dating from circa 1820 in which the family travelled across Europe. Unfortunately, during the tour, one of the Lucy children died in it when the horses were snow-bound. The gardens were landscaped circa 1760 by Capability Brown, for the sum of £525!

COMPTON WYNYATES, Tysoe, (Marquess of Northampton). The house, in pink brick, was begun by Edmund Compton in 1480 and completed by his son, William, about sixty years later. With its battlemented walls and twisted chimneys it forms a picturesque example of Tudor domestic architecture. In 1644 the house was taken from the Comptons by Roundheads, and the defensive moat was filled in. It was returned in 1646, and the family were ordered to pay a £20,000 fine.

Little of the interior has changed since the early sixteenth century. The furniture, panelled rooms and great hall are all fine examples of this period. The ceiling of Henry VIII's bedroom is original, but the other plaster ceilings may be later Jacobean work.

Pseudo-Gothic windows were added in the nineteenth century. The east front was remodelled in 1867 by Sir Matthew Wyatt, who also reconstructed the principal staircase.

Left Compton Wynyates is a fine example of Tudor domestic architecture. Notice the battlemented walls and the twisted chimneys.

69

Warwickshire

COUGHTON COURT, Alcester, (National Trust). From 1409 to 1946 Coughton was the home of the Throckmorton family, who remained loyal to the Catholic faith throughout the centuries. The house consists of a central gatehouse, built in 1509 and much restored, and two half-timbered Elizabethan wings with Georgian Gothic additions. The royal arms of Henry VIII, with dragon and greyhound supporters, portcullis and rose, are visible on the façade. The arms of the Throckmorton family, with the crest of an elephant's head over an heraldic helmet, can also be clearly seen.

The house is famous for its connection with the Gunpowder Plot of 1605. Although the family were not directly involved, they allowed the wives of the conspirators to await news of the outcome in the drawing room above the gatehouse.

Below Guy Fawkes and his friends discuss their plan to blow up the Houses of Parliament. The wives of these conspirators awaited news of the outcome of the plot in the drawing room above the gatehouse at Coughton Court.

The house suffered extensive damage during the Civil War, when the Parliamentarians bombarded it fiercely. The inhabitants vainly tried to parry the attack by hanging bedclothes over the windows, but it was finally sacked and fired. More damage followed forty-four years later in 1688, when James II fled the country. Coughton was again pillaged, and partly destroyed, when a Protestant mob from nearby Alcester rallied against the "newly erected Catholic Church." Repairs were undertaken, but the east wing was never replaced.

In 1795, the moat was filled in. It was said that the walls of the house used to rise "sheer from the water," and that "ladies used to fish leaning from their bedrooms."

The ground storey of the gate house forms the front hall, in which hangs a painted canvas called the *Tabula Eliensis*. This depicts the heads of the sovereigns from William Rufus to Elizabeth, Ely Abbey, and the arms of all the Catholic gentry imprisoned during Elizabeth's reign. Like many other Catholic relics in the house, it was hidden for safety and was discovered carefully packed away in an outbuilding.

Other interesting exhibits include a picture of Bessie Throckmorton, who became the wife of Sir Walter Raleigh; the bloodstained chemise in which Mary Queen of Scots was beheaded; a fifteenth century cope, said to have been worked by Katherine of Aragon; and the Throckmorton Coat of 1811, completed between sunrise and sunset to fulfil a wager.

Left The Throckmorton Coat was completed, to fulfil a wager, between sunrise and sunset on June 25th, 1811.

71

Warwickshire

DOLL MUSEUM, Owen's House, Castle Street, Warwick, Tel. 843, (Mrs. Joy Robinson). The museum houses the Joy Robinson collection of antique and period dolls and toys.

FARNBOROUGH HALL, near Banbury, (National Trust). The original manor was sold to Ambrose Holbeck in 1684, and he rebuilt the house with a façade seven bays wide and two storeys high. The north side was completed circa 1750.

The entrance hall displays a panelled *stucco* ceiling with Rococo motifs and busts of emperors positioned high on the walls. The original dining room has more mid-eighteenth century stucco panels, formerly framing portraits by Canaletto and Pannini which have since been replaced by copies.

In the brick walled garden is a deer larder, octagonal in shape, with *Tuscan* columns. This still contains the wheel from which game was suspended. There are also two garden temples.

HERBERT ART GALLERY AND MUSEUM, Jordan Well, Coventry, CV1 5QP, Tel. 25555, (Coventry Corporation). This art gallery and museum contains local history and industrial collections, which include early cars and cycles. There are loan art exhibitions, and the museum houses the Iliffe collection of Graham Sutherland's sketches for the great *Christ in Majesty* tapestry at Coventry Cathedral.

KENILWORTH CASTLE, Tel. Kenilworth 52078, (Department of the Environment). These red sandstone remains, celebrated in Sir Walter Scott's novel *Kenilworth*, include a massive twelfth century keep and gatehouse as well as later additional buildings. The castle was founded in 1122 by Sir Geoffrey de Clinton, Henry I's Treasurer. It passed to royal ownership under Henry

Below An engraving of Kenilworth Castle, as it appeared in 1620.

II, and then in 1244 was given to the Earl of Leicester, Simon de Montfort. But Simon rose in rebellion against Henry III and, after his defeat at Evesham, the royal army surrounded the castle. The fortifications withstood the siege, but the garrison was starved into surrender.

The castle was later turned into a palace when John of Gaunt added more living quarters. In the late sixteenth century it flourished as the home of Robert Dudley, Earl of Leicester, and Elizabeth I was a frequent visitor. Finally, in 1649, Parliament decided to destroy the castle by blowing up the keep and making breaches in its walls and towers.

Warwickshire

LEAMINGTON SPA ART GALLERY AND MUSEUM, Avenue Road, Tel. 25873, (Leamington Spa Corporation). This displays paintings by Dutch and Flemish masters, modern paintings, pottery, porcelain and glass.

LORD LEYCESTER HOSPITAL, Warwick, Tel. Warwick 42797, (Governors of the Lord Leycester Hospital). This group of buildings was one of the few to escape the great fire of 1694. It consists of the original west gate of the town, above which is built the twelfth century chapel of St. James. Its tower was added by Thomas de Beauchamp in Richard II's reign. There are also two timber-framed houses of 1383, formerly the guilds of the Holy Trinity and St. George. The guilds were dispersed in 1546, and the complex of buildings was refounded as a hospital in 1571 by Robert Dudley, Earl of Leicester, for "twelve poor and impotent persons." Since then the foundation has served retired and disabled servicemen and their wives.

The buildings have recently been restored. The former Guildhall is now a museum, and the chaplain's hall houses the Queen's Own Hussars' Regimental Museum. Below the arch, the hinge-pins on which the massive gates of the tower hung are still visible.

NUNEATON MUSEUM AND ART GALLERY, Riversley Park, Tel. 2683, (Nuneaton Corporation). The museum contains archaeological, geological and ethnographical items. There are also paintings, coins, medals, and items connected with the authoress George Eliot (1819–80) on display.

Right The Lord Leycester Hospital is made up of two timber-framed houses, the original west gate of the town of Warwick and the twelfth century chapel of St. James.

Warwickshire

PACKWOOD HOUSE, Hockley Heath, (National Trust). The main part of the Tudor timber-framed house was built by William Fetherston, who acquired the land from the Benedictine Order of Coventry. A further wing was added during the seventeenth century by John Fetherston. He also created the famous yew garden, whose clipped trees are intended to represent the Sermon on the Mount. Christ, the four apostles, and twelve disciples stand in the foreground, while the multitude cover the great lawn.

During the Civil War the family avoided damage to their house by maintaining strict neutrality. General Ireton stayed here before the Battle of Edgehill in 1642, and later Charles I was given shelter.

The interior displays many fascinating items. In the great window of the hall the arms of Queen Elizabeth and the Earls of Suffolk and Sussex are depicted. There are also two seventeenth century tapestries—*Leda and the Swan* and *David receiving the Sword of Goliath*. The dining room contains early seventeenth century Flemish glass panels. Among the pictures are a contemporary portrait of Edward VI, attributed to Hans Elworth, and an oil portrait on plaster of Charles II, attributed to Antonio Verrio (1639–1707). In Queen Margaret's room stands an "oak-stump" bedstead from Owlpen Manor, Gloucestershire, which is said to have been used by Queen Margaret of Anjou before the Battle of Tewkesbury in 1471.

The great hall was used as a barn until it was joined to the house by the addition of the long gallery in 1931–32. It now houses four tapestries. *Africa* and *America* are of Soho manufacture circa 1700, and *Alexander presenting his son to the Philosophers* is a seventeenth century Mortlake example.

RAGLEY HALL, Alcester, Tel. Alcester 2090/2455, (Marquess of Hertford). This country mansion, built in 1680, is one of the most perfect *Palladian* houses in the country. The porticos and interiors, designed by James Wyatt, were added in 1780. The decorated great hall by James Gibbs, dating from circa 1750, has a moulded plasterwork ceiling forty feet in height. The red saloon has walls papered in silk and a ceiling designed by Angelica Kauffman (1741–1804). Over the fireplace is a painting on oak panels – *The raising of Lazarus* by van Haarlems (1602).

Other attractions include paintings by Reynolds, Morland and Rubens, a valuable library, furniture, china and other *objets d'art*. The park was landscaped circa 1750 by Capability Brown.

Left The great hall at Ragley Hall.
Notice the elaborate plasterwork
ceiling which was designed by James
Gibbs circa 1750.

Warwickshire

THE ROYAL SHAKESPEARE THEATRE PICTURE GALLERY, Stratford-on-Avon. The gallery contains original theatre costumes and designs. There are portraits of William Shakespeare, and of famous actors and actresses.

SHAKESPEARE PROPERTIES, Stratford-on-Avon, Tel. 0789/4016, (Shakespeare Birthplace Trust). Anne Hathaway's Cottage, Shottery, was the home of Anne before her marriage to Shakespeare. Part of the house is fifteenth century, or earlier, while the west side dates from about 1600. The construction is varied and includes stonework, timber-framing, wattle, brick and a thatched roof. Exhibits are interesting but not all contemporary with Shakespeare.

Hall's Croft, Stratford, was the home of Shakespeare's daughter, Susanna, and her husband Dr. John Hall. Furniture and period exhibits are displayed. Adjoining the house is a walled garden.

Mary Arden's House, Wilmcote, is a Tudor farmhouse, three miles north-west of Stratford. It is reputed to be the home of Shakespeare's mother, although this identification only dates from 1798. Folk-life exhibits are displayed in the house, while the barns contain agricultural implements.

At New Place, Chapel Street, Stratford, the foundations of the house to which Shakespeare went in 1610 are preserved in the replica of an Elizabethan knot garden.

Shakespeare was born in Henley Street, Stratford. The half-timbered house, which is early sixteenth century, contains many Shakespeare relics and period furnishings. In Shakespeare's day the property was two separate buildings—one the family home, the other an adjoining warehouse used by Shakespeare's father John, who was a glover and wool dealer.

Below An early nineteenth century Staffordshire figure of Shakespeare.

78

UPTON HOUSE, Edgehill, (National Trust). The original country mansion of James II's reign was enlarged in 1927. The house displays Brussels tapestries, Sèvres porcelain and a large collection of paintings from all the major European Schools. Of particular interest are *The Adoration of the Magi* by Jerome Bosch and the Raeburn portrait of the young Clanranald Brothers.

Left This early Tudor bedstead can be seen at Hall's Croft, the home of Shakespeare's daughter.
Below The Adoration of the Magi by Jerome Bosch.

Warwickshire

WARWICK CASTLE, Warwick, Tel. Warwick 45421, (Lord Brooke). The earliest stronghold on this site, which overlooks the river Avon, is attributed to the daughter of King Alfred, Ethelfleda. The present castle, however, consists of a fourteenth to fifteenth century enclosure within which is a seventeenth century dwelling.

The chief features of the medieval castle are the two lofty towers, Caesar's and Guy's. The gatehouse is of the same period. The castle was owned by the Beauchamps, Earls of Warwick, who were in turn succeeded by Richard Neville, the "Kingmaker." Under Henry VIII the castle and earldom passed to Robert Dudley, but it reverted to the Crown when he was beheaded in 1552. It was presented to Sir Fulke Greville, the first Lord Brooke, by James I.

The interior was largely rebuilt in the late seventeenth century, and again circa 1770 following a fire. Although the great hall is part of the original castle, its roof is nineteenth century. Exhibits include a collection of armour, including Oliver Cromwell's helmet, and a chest belonging to Izaak Walton. The cedar room, which is late seventeenth century, is hung with Van Dyck's portraits of Cavalier leaders. The cedar panelling is of 1871. Two late seventeenth century ceilings, in Queen Anne's bedroom and the blue boudoir, survived a further fire of 1871. The library, however, was redesigned in Italian Renaissance style. The gardens were laid out in the mid-eighteenth century by Capability Brown.

WARWICK COUNTY MUSEUM, Market Place, Warwick, Tel. 43431 Ext. 329, (Warwickshire County Council). The museum is housed in the Market Hall, built in 1670, and serves all Warwickshire. There are natural history, history, archaeological and geological collections which include the finest series of British fossil

Above The lofty and imposing Caesar's Tower at Warwick Castle, from an engraving of 1814.

amphibians from the *Triassic* period. There is a museum education department.

ST. JOHN'S HOUSE, Tel. 43431 Ext. 132. This seventeenth century house and garden contain the folk life, craft and costume displays of the Warwick County Museum. The Museum of the Royal Warwickshire Regiment is housed upstairs.

Worcestershire

ALMONRY MUSEUM, Vine Street, Evesham, (Vale of Evesham Historical Society). The museum contains Romano-British, Anglo-Saxon, medieval and monastic remains. There are agricultural implements and local history material.

THE AVONCROFT MUSEUM OF BUILDINGS LTD, Stoke Prior, near Bromsgrove, Tel. Bromsgrove 31363. This museum was set up to stimulate an interest in buildings of historic or architectural merit, and to prevent their destruction. At the moment the museum has a fifteenth century timber-framed merchant's house, a windmill, nail and chainmakers' workshops, an eighteenth century granary and reconstructions of

Iron Age huts. The major exhibit is the restored fourteenth century Guesten Hall roof. This will eventually be incorporated in a building which will provide space for activities such as exhibitions and lectures.

BEWDLEY MUSEUM, The Shambles, Load Street, Tel. 3573, (Bewdley Corporation). The museum is housed in the late eighteenth century Shambles or butchers' market. The museum's emphasis is on the former crafts of Bewdley and the Wyre Forest region. These include horn making, bark peeling, tanning, saddlery, making brassware and pewtering. There is also a reconstructed ropewalk, and workshops of a cooper and basketmaker. A living crafts exhibition area has been set up. The Wyre Forest gallery contains information on the natural history of the area, and an agricultural gallery traces the traditional processes of the farming year.

CITY MUSEUM AND ART GALLERY, WORCESTER, Foregate Street, Tel. 22154, (Worcester Corporation). The museum has expanding collections of folk life material, archaeology, geology and natural history. These illustrate man and his environment in the Severn valley region, with particular reference to the city of Worcester. The art gallery has both temporary and permanent exhibitions.

TUDOR HOUSE FOLK MUSEUM, Friar Street. In this museum there are displays illustrating the social history and domestic life of the city of Worcester.

Above The Danzey Green windmill is re-erected at Avoncroft Museum. The skirt and tail-pole wheel have now been installed.

Left This Iron Age hut has been reconstructed at Avoncroft Museum of Buildings.

Worcestershire

THE COMMANDERY, Worcester, (H. D. Little-bury). A pre-Reformation hospital of St. Wulstan, which was the headquarters of an order of Knights or "Commanders," occupied this site from 1085 to 1540. Ownership passed to Richard Morrison in 1541, and he built the present Tudor house. The great hall is impressive with its oriel windows and stained-glass bird, wheat-ear and flower motifs. There is an Elizabethan staircase which leads to upper rooms with Jacobean panelling. Some early sixteenth century wall paintings depict the Crucifixion, the Weighing of Souls and the Martyrdom of Becket and Erasmus. In September 1651, the Commandery was chosen as the Royalist headquarters under the command of the Duke of Hamilton, who dined with the King in the great hall on the night before the Battle of Worcester. The next day,

Below A reconstructed Black Country forge at Dudley Museum and Art Gallery.

according to Clarendon, the Duke had his leg "broken short off" by a cannon ball. He refused amputation and died the day after.

DUDLEY MUSEUM AND ART GALLERY, St. James's Road, Dudley, Tel. 56321, (Dudley Corporation). This museum contains a geological gallery which is noted for its local limestone and coal measure fossils. These collections link up with the geological nature trail at the nearby Wren's Nest Nature Reserve. Close by, the Brooke Robinson Museum shows fine art and occasional temporary exhibitions. An open air Black Country Museum is being developed on an historic site and will eventually cover ten acres.

BRIERLEY HILL GLASS MUSEUM AND ART GALLERY, Moor Street, Tel. 56321. This houses a fine collection of local Stourbridge and foreign glass, together with reference literature. There are occasional temporary exhibitions.

THE DYSON PERRINS MUSEUM OF WORCESTER PORCELAIN, The Royal Porcelain Works, Severn Street, Worcester, Tel. 22154, (The Dyson Perrins Museum Trust). The museum contains the finest and most comprehensive collection of old Worcester porcelain in the world.

THE GREYFRIARS, Worcester, (National Trust). This timber-framed house was built for the Franciscan friary which then adjoined it, probably as the guest house, in about 1480. The most impressive room, which contains a late sixteenth century plaster frieze, is on the first floor and is reached by an Elizabethan staircase.

Above A tureen and cover takes the form of a partridge sitting on its nest. This was made in Worcester circa 1770 and would have originally cost about seven shillings. It is now on show at the Dyson Perrins Museum and is worth about £1,000.

Right The great hall at Worcester Commandery. It was here that Charles II dined with the Duke of Hamilton on the night before the Battle of Worcester in 1651.

85

Worcestershire

THE GUILDHALL, Worcester, Tel. 23471, (Worcester Corporation). This was built between 1721 and 1723 by a pupil of Christopher Wren, Thomas White of Worcester. The façade is particularly fine. Statues of Charles I and Charles II flank the entrance, and above the doorway is the carved head of Cromwell nailed by the ears—a grim reminder that Cromwell's actual head remained at Westminster Hall for twenty years. Between the central windows stands a statue of Queen Anne. The loyalty of the city is summed up in its motto *Semper Fidelis*—"Always Loyal." Further figures are depicted above the cornice—Justice, Peace, Plenty, Chastisement and Hercules.

The building was restored in the nineteenth century by Sir Gilbert Scott. On display inside are corporation plate, ceremonial swords and four eighteenth century maces.

HANBURY HALL, near Droitwich, (National Trust). The hall, built about 1700 in red brick by Thomas Vernon, is a fully proportioned example of the period in Wren's style. Off the spacious entrance hall lies the restrained Baroque staircase, with its decorated balusters

Left The Guildhall at Worcester. Notice the carved head of Cromwell above the doorway and the statues of Queen Anne, Charles I and Charles II.

built by Thornhill about 1710. The walls and ceilings are painted with large scenes, including *The Battle for the Arms of Achilles* and *The Assembly of the Gods*, which depicts a cherub holding a portrait of Dr. Sacheverell about to be torn to pieces by Furies. Sacheverell was an Anglican minister whose violently outrageous views brought him to trial in 1710. There are other Thornhill paintings on the panelled ceilings in the long room. This also contains a carved wooden overmantel in Rococo style circa 1750, which provides a contrast with the Jacobean overmantel on the ground floor.

Right Dr. Sacheverell was a very controversial figure in the early eighteenth century. This design for a playing card shows him surrounded by well-wishers, while "The Assembly of Gods" at Hanbury Hall depicts a cherub holding a portrait of Sacheverell about to be torn to pieces by Furies.

Others would Swell with Pride, if thus cares'd, But he bears humble Thoughts within his Breast

Worcestershire

HARTLEBURY CASTLE, Hartlebury, Tel. 214, (Lord Bishop of Worcester). The present building, approached by an avenue of limes which were planted by Charles II's chaplain, Bishop Stillingfleet, dates from 1675. There are some eighteenth century additions. The site has been the residence of the Bishops of Worcester for over a thousand years. The fortifications of the earlier castle, begun about 1255 by Bishop Cantelupe, Lord Chancellor, are visible at the base of the round north-west tower. Part of the moat survives at the rear of the building. During the Civil War the castle fell into Parliamentarian hands, and it was used as a prison for Royalists until its demolition in 1646.

The state rooms include the great hall and portrait gallery, and an eighteenth century Rococo saloon. The staircase, which has heavy balusters, dates from 1680 and is typical of the period. The library, installed in 1782 by Bishop Hurd, displays books in original eighteenth century bookcases.

HARVINGTON HALL, near Kidderminster, Tel. Chaddesley Corbett 267, (Roman Catholic Archdiocese of Birmingham). This moated Tudor house, which incorporates some earlier building, was probably constructed by John Packington. Fragments of paintings dating back to the end of the fifteenth century have been discovered beneath the whitewash, but more impressive are the six large pictures of *The Nine Worthies* and *David slaying Goliath*, which date from about 1570.

The house had strong Catholic loyalties, and a number of priest holes and secret passages were constructed to enable priests to escape seventeenth century persecution. One priest, the Blessed John Wall, escaped for twelve years. He was finally caught and executed for treason at Worcester in 1679. He is reputed to have said to his executioner, who had politely asked him to indicate when he was prepared, "I will give you no sign: do it when you will."

KIDDERMINSTER MUSEUM AND ART GALLERY, Market Street, Tel. 62832, (Kidderminster Corporation). Small, permanent, art collections are on display in the museum, and loan exhibitions are held. The museum holds material belonging to the Kidderminster and District Archaeological and Historical Society.

Below The priest hole under the stairs at Harvington Hall. A number of secret holes and passages were built in the house to help Catholic priests escape from persecution in the seventeenth century.

Worcestershire

WITLEY COURT, Great Witley, (Department of the Environment). The present ruined building, roofless and overgrown since it was destroyed by fire in 1937, was once the home of Lord Foley. It was erected in the early eighteenth century on a site purchased by his grandfather, Thomas Foley, with money from his iron works. Restorations, and additions to the original building, were made by the Earl of Dudley in the nineteenth century.

Particularly impressive are the remains of two fountains to the rear and side of the ruined court. The

Below The Perseus Fountain at Witley Court. The rearing horse is twenty-six feet high and was sculpted by James Forsyth circa 1860.

fountain of Perseus and Andromeda is one of the largest pieces of sculpture in Europe. The rearing horse is twenty-six feet in height and is sculpted in the grand Baroque manner by James Forsyth. Adjoining the ruined court is the chapel (now Great Witley Parish Church), which was consecrated in 1735. It is a surprising and lavish example of the Rococo style, and was originally built to display the treasures of the Foleys. The total decor was bought from the house of the first Duke of Chandos in Edgware. The windows were painted between 1719 and 1721 by Joshua Price, from designs by Francisco Slater. The painted ceilings and panels are by Antonio Belluci, and the three largest works depict the Ascension, the Nativity and the Descent.

The church also contains one of the largest eighteenth century funerary monuments in England. The monument to Lord Foley, who died in 1732, was the work of Rysbrack. It depicts a family group, with the Baron reclining, his wife sitting with a child on her left, and a young man and girl standing above. All the figures are clad in loose drapery.

WORCESTERSHIRE COUNTY MUSEUM,

Hartlebury, near Kidderminster, Tel. Hartlebury 416, (Worcestershire County Council Education Department). The museum is housed in the north wing of the Bishop of Worcester's palace. It depicts the archaeology, social history, crafts and industries of the county. Among other exhibits there are furniture, costume, toys, domestic equipment and glass. Outside there is a restored cider mill, a blacksmith's forge, and horse-drawn vehicles including gypsy caravans. There are also a picnic area and a nature reserve. This museum has an education department.

Worcestershire County Museum has a wide range of exhibits which include an eighteenth century costume display *(top)* and a bow-top caravan.

WOLVERHAMPTON TEACHERS COLLEGE LIBRARY

Glossary

ALABASTER A type of white stone used for sculpture.

BALUSTER A short column or pillar, often supporting the rail of a staircase.

BAROQUE An ornate style of architecture, used mainly in the early eighteenth century.

BYGONES Objects from the relatively recent past.

CANOPY Projection or hood, over a pulpit for example.

CASTELLATED Having battlements like a castle.

CERAMICS Pottery and porcelain.

CLASSICAL The architecture of ancient Greece and Rome, or any style inspired by it.

CORINTHIAN The most elaborate of the three Greek orders of architecture.

CORNICE The moulding running round a room where walls and ceiling meet, or any group of mouldings which crown a building.

CRUCK A pair of bent trees used to support the roofs of early houses and barns.

DIORAMA A spectacular painting in which natural processes, such as sunrise, are produced by the use of light and colour.

DORIC The simplest of the Greek orders of architecture.

ENAMELS Small copper objects, such as snuff boxes, which were decorated with a kind of opaque glass.

ETHNOGRAPHY The science describing the races of man.

FACADE The front of a building.

FINIAL An ornament finishing off the top of an architectural feature, such as a gable or canopy.

FRIEZE A band, frequently ornamental, which comes below the cornice.

GEOLOGY The study of the earth's crust.

GOTHIC The architecture of the Middle Ages. The style was revived in the eighteenth century.

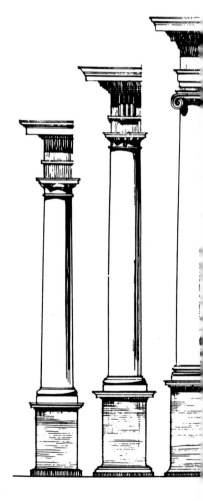

Doric   Tuscan   Ioni

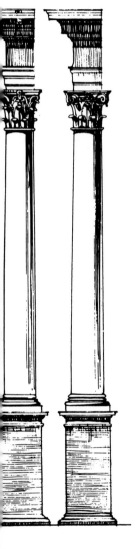

Orders of columns

Corinthian

HAMMERBEAM ROOF Roof supported by a beam projecting at right angles from the top of the walls.

IONIC One of the Greek orders of architecture.

ITALIANATE An architectural style of Italian appearance.

JACOBEAN The architecture of the reigns of James I and Charles I (1603–1649).

JAPANNING The art of lacquering metal goods.

LATEX Milky fluid of a plant.

LAVATORIUM A bowl or basin for washing the hands.

NORMAN A style of architecture, characterized by rounded arches, which dominated the late eleventh and twelfth centuries.

NEWEL POST The principal post of a wooden staircase where the flight meets the landing.

PALLADIAN A style of architecture based on the ideas of Andrea Palladio (1508–1580).

PINNACLE A small slender ornamental turret.

RENAISSANCE Architectural style based on the study and adaptation of classical designs.

RESTORATION PERIOD The years immediately after 1660, when Charles II was restored to the throne.

ROCOCO A flamboyant style, derived from Baroque, which was in vogue during the eighteenth century.

ROUNDEL A small, decorative, circular ornament.

SAMPLER A piece of needlework or embroidery with texts and alphabets worked in different stitches.

SOLAR The upper private living-room of a medieval or Tudor house.

STUCCO Plasterwork.

TRACERY Ornamental open work, especially at the top of a Gothic window.

TREFOIL An ornamental design often found in tracery. Similar to a clover leaf without a stalk.

TRIASSIC A geological period which began 225,000,000 years ago and lasted for about 35,000,000 years.

TUSCAN An architectural order of Roman origin, plain in style and similar to the Doric.

Further Reading

M. & M. Hardwick, *Writers' Houses* (J. M. Dent, 1968).

Historic Houses, Castles and Gardens in Great Britain and Ireland (ABC Travel Guides, published yearly).

Museums and Galleries in Great Britain and Ireland (ABC Travel Guides, published yearly).

A. L. Osborne, *The Country Life Pocket Guide to English Domestic Architecture* (Country Life, 1967).

J. Penoyre & M. Ryan, *The Observer's Book of Architecture* (Frederick Warne, 1970).

Treasures of Britain (Drive Publications, 1968).

H. Thorold, *Derbyshire: a Shell Guide* (Faber & Faber, 1972).

W. G. Hoskins, *Leicestershire: a Shell Guide* (Faber & Faber, 1970).

Arthur Mee, *Nottinghamshire* (Hodder & Stoughton, 1970).

M. Moulder, *Shropshire: a Shell Guide* (Faber & Faber, 1972).

Vincent Waite, *Shropshire Hill Country* (J. M. Dent, 1970).

Arthur Mee, *Staffordshire* (Hodder & Stoughton, 1971).

N. Pevsner & A. Wedgwood, *The Buildings of England: Warwickshire* (Penguin, 1966).

Arthur Mee, *Worcestershire* (Hodder & Stoughton, 1968).

N. Pevsner, *The Buildings of England: Worcestershire* (Penguin, 1968).

Index

Picture Credits

The authors and Publishers wish to thank the following for their kind
permission to reproduce copyright illustrations on the pages mentioned:
Avoncroft Museum of Buildings, 83; the Barsted Collection, 79; Berrow's
Newspapers, 90; the *Birmingham Evening Mail*, 67; Birmingham Museum
and Art Gallery, 13, 14, 15, 18, 19, 21, 44, 64, 66, 67 (top); the *Birmingham
Post*, 17; Cheddleton Flint Mill Industrial Heritage Trust, 55; the City
Museum and Art Gallery, Stoke-on-Trent, 60, 61; the Controller of Her
Majesty's Stationery Office (Crown copyright), 50–51, 51; *Country Life*,
40–41, 63; Derby Museums and Art Gallery, 23; Dudley Museum and
Art Gallery, 84; Dyson Perrins Museum, 85; A. F. Kersting, 38–39, 47, 71,
77, 86; Leicester Museum and Art Gallery, 9 (top); Lord Leycester
Hospital, jacket, 74–75; the Mansell Collection, 26, 27; the National
Monuments Record, 68, 81, 85; the National Portrait Gallery, 30, 43,
53; Nottingham City Museum and Art Gallery, 35; Nottingham
Public Libraries, 34; Photografis, 82; *Punch, frontispiece;* the Shakespeare
Birthplace Trust, 78, 79; the Sir Benjamin Stone Collection of Photographs,
Birmingham Public Libraries, 72–73, 89; Staffordshire County Museum,
58 (photo by J. F. Kersting), 59; R. W. Tennent, 9 (bottom); Transglobe
Film Distributors Ltd., 37; the Trustees of the British Museum, 48–49, 87;
the Waterways Museum, British Waterways Board, 33; Weidenfeld and
Nicolson (drawing by Leonora Ison in "Architecture in England"),
92–93; Jeremy Whitaker, 25; Worcestershire County Museum, 91.
Other illustrations appearing in this book are the property of Wayland
Picture Library.